THE NOVA COLLECTIVE

Practical Life Lessons From a Girl
Who's Been Through Some Sh-t

SYENOVIA LESESNE

WHERE DO I START?

Question. Where does a girl who never thought she'd be writing a book, start writing a book? Answer: the beginning, I guess. Everyone has experienced, is experiencing and will experience different challenges. I didn't start this project intending to convince you that as long as you're a 'good' person, bad things won't happen. The purpose of this book is to promote positive thinking, and to reassure every reader that no matter how bleak things may seem, things are ALWAYS working exactly the way that they are supposed to.

This world, and the hearts of some of the people in it are messed up! Today more than ever, it is imperative that you get, and KEEP your mind right. I have found that this is a helluva (issa word, just keep reading) lot easier when you keep a positive mindset. As you turn the pages, you'll notice that this book is broken up into seven sections. Each section contains a series of notes designed to encourage, motivate, uplift, reassure and gently remind you about life's every day challenges (which we will now refer to as 'lessons'…how's that for a thought shift)?

Now listen! At present, I am a 31 year old single mother of two children, ages 7 and 5. I'm still young, still learning, still trying to find my way! I do not claim to have all of the answers. I'm just a girl who's been through, and grown through some sh-t. That said, my hope is that you'll find the contents of this project helpful, that you'll refer to it as often as you need to when you need a 'pick-me-up'...or confirmation that you'll be okay. I'm not saying things will be easy, most times the 'getting through' SUCKS. But, as long as you refuse to stay down, you can get back up.

Oh, and I suppose now is as good a time as any, to thank you for thinking enough of me to spend your hard earned coins on a copy of this book. Many, many thanks, a trillion times over for support-ing the dream. With love, the truest, the deepest, most thoroughest kind, Syen-ovia.

Section One:

KEEP YOUR HEAD UP, AND YOUR CHIN PARALLEL TO THE FLOOR; YOU'LL WALK RIGHT INTO A WALL IF YOU DON'T.

"Mistakes are okay. A confident person is someone who has made and learned from a million mistakes."

Show me an 'expert' who never made a mistake, and I'll show you a liar. In my opinion, experience is the BEST teacher. And the only way to gain experience is to f–ck up, ALOT, and then learn from your mistakes. After all, what are mistakes, but an opportunity to try again, and get it right the next time?

"Start; keep going and, don't stop going until you're done."

I sat on this project for years! But for close friends, and a strong social media following (I don't have hundreds of thousands of followers, but the one's I've got are true), this book would still be sitting in my lime green composition notebook. If you've got something that you want to accomplish, I encourage you to start RIGHT now. Six months from now, you'll be glad that you did. It's easier to gain and maintain momentum once you get going, but you've got to get going first.

"If you fall down, get back up."

Don't worry about how yesterday turned out; each day is a new chance to start over BETTER, to find your groove and succeed. If you start and fail to stick to something, start over. Don't give up, START OVER. And keep starting over until you don't have to anymore.

"Don't dwell on your mistakes. Nothing good will come of that. Focus on the recovery instead."

Don't spend too much time licking your wounds (mistakes, disappointments, etc), sulking and feeling sorry for yourself. Bandage those b-tches up, identify the lesson(s) learned, take a deep breath, and then GET BACK UP.

"No matter what things may look like, feel like, sound like,....PRESS your way through."

Throwing in the towel is exactly what the enemy wants you to do. If you give in, you'll feel defeated, discouraged and less than the champion that you are. No matter the circumstance, press your way through. When you come out on the other end, you'll be stronger, wiser and feel better about yourself.

"Struggle is conditioning for prosperity."

Life is all about balance. You've got to take the good, with the bad. Trust me, you'll be okay. If it could have killed you, you'd be dead already.

"Half a step forward is better than no steps at all, are better than half a step back."

Strive for progress, not perfection. Tracking your progress will keep you motivated. Slow progress is STILL progress! The first step toward making PROGRESS is, to start NOW. Whatchu waitin' on?

"Progress precedes perfection; keep going."

You gone have to get it wrong a few times just to get it right. Every attempt is progress. Enough progressive attempts will eventually yield perfection...according to YOUR standards. Those who are meant to catch your message will so, don't worry about trying to please everyone.

"If at first you don't succeed, try, try again."

Acknowledge yesterday's opportunities, identify your lesson(s), then use what you've learned to start over BETTER tomorrow.

"Like a runner in a race, find YOUR pace, stay consistent and don't stop going until you've reached the end."

Don't overextend yourself by getting caught up in how quickly everybody else 'appears to be' moving. You'll end up too fatigued to finish YOUR race that way. Instead, keep your focus. Don't waste time or energy looking left, or right. Find YOUR pace, and run YOUR face, in anticipation of YOUR win.

"Don't call them 'problems'...call them 'challenges' instead."

The word 'problems' has a negative connotation. People associate problems with struggle, and a slew of other negative feelings. When you replace the word 'problems' with 'challenges',...you're taking on a PROFOUND thought shift. Now, difficult situations no longer seem impossible to overcome; instead, you now feel empowered to defy or overcome the obstacle in front of you.

"Stop worrying; it does you absolutely no good."

Worrying can take years off of your life. This is a fact; if you don't believe me, Google that sh–t. A little anxiety about the unknown is normal; BUT extreme fear about things that haven't even happened yet is just crazy. So, stop worrying today and, just do. If you nail it, GOOD. If you f–ck up, that's GOOD too. Write down every lesson you learned, and then prove to yourself that you can do 'it' right. Did you catch that? I said don't worry about proving 'them' wrong. F–ck them; prove yourself right instead. Life is easier to live when you don't worry about how the story ends.

"The person you sought help from is entitled to say No."

It doesn't mean he/she doesn't support your shine. Sometimes 'no' means I love you enough to tell you 'no' because I may not follow through on my commitment. I love you enough to tell you 'no' before you go before the world and embarrass yourself. You ought to be thankful for those who are honest enough to tell you no. Don't get mad, get focused and get busy instead.

"Your odds at winning are increased exponentially if you are brave enough try."

You should choose to bet on you. This is easier to do when you believe in yourself. I think part of the reason that I sat on this project so long is because I didn't believe in myself. I didn't think I was a 'writer.' It wasn't until I resolved to be about all that I spoke about, that I decided to get serious about becoming a published author. And, lo and behold,. . . when I got serious sh-t started happening.

"Sometimes sh–t has to happen so that a shift can happen."

No matter how uncomfortable, you should find solace in the fact that it's all part of YOUR process. I learned life changing lessons when I was the most uncomfortable. Failed friendships, failed relationships, taught me to be more cautious, and in doing so, I became a better judge of character. Those situations also heightened my awareness of self. When I look back, I realize that some of the people I let in my life, didn't deserve to be there. Being there wasn't their fault though; after all, they couldn't exist where I didn't allow them to. Geeeezzzz, when you look at it that way, you feel crazy powerful right? If you don't, go back and reread the last two sentences until you do. I know good and damn well, that was a GOODT word.

"You may have made some mis-takes, and in doing so, bit off more than you could chew. Don't be afraid to put whatever you're working on down. "

At one stage in my life, I was the queen of overextending myself. I said 'Yes' even if it was something I knew I didn't want to do. If you are this type of person, you should break this bad habit ASAP. It may cost you some relationships that you THOUGHT were solid; but, a relationship (platonic or otherwise) that is ended because you chose to care for self wasn't REAL from the jump. Real relationships are not always convenient; but, they withstand the test of time because they are honest and understanding. A REAL ONE GONE UNDERSTAND.

"Your foundation is fortified brick, by brick."

Some days you'll lay fifty bricks with ease. Other days it will be a struggle to lay five. Don't stop laying them though. EVERY brick makes your foundation stronger. EVERY. BRICK.

Section Two:

TAKE THE HIGH ROAD. THE RIDE WON'T ALWAYS BE EASY; BUT, THERE WILL BE LESS TRAFFIC. AND YOU WON'T HAVE TO WORRY ABOUT ANYBODY SWERVING INTO YOUR LANE.

"Don't let someone else's behavior interrupt your inner peace."

Holding grudges is like allowing a person to live in your thoughts rent free! Move to evict, and let that person (and the mess that comes along with them) GO! The idea behind this is peace. And PEACE is a whole vibe.

"All things are working for your good."

Every experience, positive or negative is a lesson; an opportunity to learn from every thing you did right, and more importantly, everything that you did wrong. So you see, even when things are f-cked up, they are STILL good.

"Adversity exposes weak bonds."

It's exhausting to spend energy asking 'why this friendship ended' or 'why this relationship ended.' Instead of questioning why separation was necessary, give thanks for the exposure of weak bonds. 'Adulting' can be difficult enough; I don't know about you, but I don't have time to question who's down for me, and who ain't.

"Nothing in life will always live up to your expectations. Others will fail you; again, and again. Forgive and drive on."

It's important to note that, YOU will never always live up to your OWN expectations either! So it's unrealistic to think that you'll always be able to live up to someone else's! The sooner you forgive yourself and others, the sooner you are healed. Disappointment just isn't worth holding on to.

"No win is worth the cheat."

Integrity over all. The. End.

"Not everyone will be willing to help you. It just is, what it is."

The reality is, nobody is obligated to help you either. Some won't help because they aren't interested. Others won't help because they don't have the means. Some won't help because they simply do not want to see you win. Recognize which category 'some' falls in, and then focus all of your energy on nurturing the relationships you've built with those who have always been willing.

"You don't have to win every argument."

Agree to disagree; and then, move on. Forget about 'winning.' MUTUAL UNDERSTANDING is, and should always be the ultimate goal.

"Treat people BETTER than they treat you."

You could have said 'Yes' a million times before; but, when the sh-t hits the fan, everybody you said yes to, will only remember when you said 'No.' This is not to say that you should be a 'Yes' man. I told you in Section One that's not where it's at. What I'm saying is this. One day you'll have to answer for every decision you made. If you can help, you should do so willingly with a gracious heart. God will honor your good-doing. Trends come and go but being kind will never go out of style.

"Karma doesn't need your help; she can handle her business all by herself."

If a person doesn't do right by you, stay out of it. His or her punishment should not come at the hands of you. The only being with that kind of authority is DIVINE. Don't worry about getting back at the people who have crossed you; focus your energy on something more productive. Karma is an expert at what she does. Keep your hands and face clean, and let her do her job.

"Be what they can't be; YOU."

In a world chock full of carbon copies, it's easy to get lost in what everybody else is doing. Different is more attractive. You are different because you aren't them. Keep being you, like only YOU know how.

"If you want the last laugh, all you have to do is keep walking a positive walk."

Keep motivating and encouraging yourself and others around you; and, be PATIENT. The last part of the previous sentence isn't about get back; it's about growth. After while, what once bothered and ate away at your peace of mind, will have little to no effect on you at all. I know this because I've experienced this.

"Take the high road; that's how you keep the upper hand."

I know, this is easier said than done. But, hear me out though. Think back on a time when you were upset and acted out. Maybe you said some things that you know you had no business saying. Maybe you did some things that you know you had no business doing. Think back on the remorse you felt after letting your emotions get the best of you. Think back on the remorse you felt after having to deal with the consequences of your words and/or actions. That can be a terrible feeling. One way to mitigate the risk associated with remorse is to choose the high road. You may walk away feeling like 'damn I should have given him/her a piece of my mind' but, YOU WON'T REGRET EXERCISING SELF CONTROL.

Section

Three:

LOVE THYSELF, AND TO THINE OWN SELF STAY TRUE.

"There are two types of people in the world; those who propel you forward, and those who don't."

There is no in between here. It's a black and white matter; no grey. If you create a grey space to preserve relationships that are taking you no where physically, spiritually and/or emotionally, you're doing yourself a disservice. Take inventory of your closest relationships; and, commence to spring cleaning.

Repeat after me: "I am not for everybody; and, that's okay."

Not everybody will love your idiosyncrasies. Not everybody will get you. But, everybody shouldn't matter when you know that YOU'RE enough. The people who are supposed to get you will. Don't get so hung up on everybody who doesn't get you. Focus all of your energy on the people who do. Therein lie your blessings.

"When a person shows you who they are, do yourself a favor and believe them."

More often than not, the signs are always there. We just choose to overlook them. I'm encouraging you not to fall victim to this trap. When a person shows you who they are, BELIEVE THEM. If he shows you that he is a liar, do not expect the truth from him. If she shows you that she is not loyal, it would be foolish to expect loyalty from her, The sooner you adopt this thought shift, the sooner your headache will go away.

"Feed yourself first."

When taken at face value, this statement sounds incredibly selfish doesn't it? But, stay with me. It's actually more SELFLESS than anything. I say that because one must feed his or herself to be well enough to feed anyone else. This quote is rooted in SELF CARE. You can, and do take care of others, because you take care of yourself.

"Love yourself. Forgive yourself. Be true to yourself."

Be transparent with yourself. Be honest with yourself too. Be patient with yourself. Be empathetic with yourself. If not you, then who?

"Five different people will have five different opinions about whatever it is that you're doing."

This world is chaotic. Trying to please everybody will leave you exhausted. Keep your focus on whatever works for you; and DO THAT WELL.

"You are worthy."

Whatever you did yesterday is done. If you woke up this morning determined to make today better than yesterday, you are worthy of having a better day. If you woke up this morning and decided that you wanted to make a MAJOR lifestyle change, you are worthy of being taken seriously the moment you declared that change. Don't let anyone make you feel less than. YOU ARE WORTHY.

"Evolving can (and often will) be misconstrued as acting funny."

Keep growing anyway. The reality is, we all grow in different ways at different speeds; and, that's okay. We grow together, we grow apart, we grow rapidly, we grow at a snails pace, etc. If you're evolving, you're growing. And, growth is progression. Don't let anyone who can't keep up, slow you down.

"If you want to be a well-rounded individual, you'll have to choose to never stop learning."

Continuous learning means continuous growing. And, continuous growth yields progression toward the best version of yourself. I don't know about you, but I want to be 'all that and a bag of chips forever' LOL. So if you feel like I feel, choose to NEVER stop learning.

"Learn to complete yourself; you are ENOUGH."

Quick math lesson: one half, plus one half, equals ONE WHOLE. One whole, plus one whole, equals TWO WHOLES. Did you catch that? When a whole person joins another whole person, you get TWO WHOLE PEOPLE. Nobody is deficient.

Section Four:

SIMPLIFY YOUR LIST OF THINGS TO DO.

"Choose QUALITY over quantity."

In today's social media charged world, don't make the mistake of letting your number of followers determine your self worth. What's the point in having 100K followers who don't motivate you, or put a dime in your pocket? That's like having a car that doesn't run.

"Stay busy AND productive."

Too much free time is a bad thing. In retrospect, I realize that I entertained a lot of useless connections, conversations, and the like, simply because I did not have enough going on. When you are busy, you don't have time to engage certain people and or situations. When you are productive, you attract other productive people; people who are making moves,...and when you're MOVING, things start happening.

"Stop putting yourself down."

Loving yourself enough to stop putting yourself down will make a profound difference in the way you view yourself and, life in general. If you refuse to put yourself down, you choose to believe in yourself. When you choose to believe in yourself, you create a better quality of life. It's like a domino effect with only positive side effects.

"Choose happy, and then BE HAPPY."

We've all heard the phrase 'life is 10% what actually happens, and 90% how we choose to deal with what happens.' This means each day we are empowered. We may not have any control over what the day holds, BUT WE HAVE COMPLETE CONTROL over how we choose to deal with every obstacle thrown our way. I can't speak for you; but, for me, life just feels better knowing that I am empowered to CHOOSE.

"Focus. Plan. Execute. Repeat."

This is a simple formula for getting sh-t done. Carrying this out won't always be easy. I won't sit here and tell you that lie; BUT, if you'll press past every day you don't feel like handling business, you won't regret doing so.

"Create your idea of success; and then, spend your days being successful."

Don't let this one or that one tell you that you can't be successful. Don't give anyone that kind of influence over your life.

"Instead of living every day like it's your last, try living every day walking in optimism, expecting tomorrow to be better instead."

Even though I understand the idea behind the notion of living every day like it's your last, that way of thinking can be harmful. Instead of living like you'll die tomorrow, live expecting to be BETTER tomorrow. It's about living the best version of yourself.

"F-ck with the kind of people who keep their promises, even when they're mad."

You just ought to be the type of person too. When you run across these type, make sure to handle these relationships with utmost care. These type of people are precious; scattered few, far and in between.

"Collaboration over competition."

When we work together, we cover more ground.

"Don't expect to start and be perfect."

That's not realistic. Instead, find your starting point, then start small, and put together a plan to get back on track when you miss the mark. The last part of this formula is SO IMPORTANT. When your plan breaks down, you need a plan to recover so you don't give up.

"Don't let that sh–t go; talk that sh–t out instead."

When something goes down and you choose to 'sweep it under the rug' instead of talking about how the situation left you feeling, you plant a seed for more conflict. Good communication will save you a million and three headaches; don't let sh–t go. Talk that sh–t out instead.

"Struggle. Recover. Prosper."

No one is always up; I don't care what your Instagram feed is telling you. Social media is smoke and mirrors; the content is scripted, and edited a million times over...and, that ain't real life. IN REAL LIFE, we'll all struggle at some point or another. BUT, the wonderful thing is, we can recover from every setback, and prosper too,...if we'll just fix our minds to do so. Struggle. Recover. Prosper. It won't be easy, but you should find a way.

"Be open and available to others."

In my opinion, this is the most genuine kind of love. In addition to being open and available, you ought to be affirming to others too. Sometimes all we need to get going again, is a gentle reminder that we can handle whatever life throws at us. The wonderful thing about practicing this lil lesson is, the gift is two-sided; both the giver and receiver benefit from this exchange.

"Choose SIMPLE over complicated."

Complicated doesn't always equal better; BUT it will always breed stress. And, stress can take years off of your life. Choose simple over complicated. Oh, it should be noted that simple won't always be easy...sometimes, the simplest decisions are the MOST difficult to make and/or stick to.

"Stop making other people's problems your problems."

Some of the sh-t we let weigh us down, isn't even ours to carry. Stop making other people's problems your problems. Stop tolerating less than you deserve. Do yourself the biggest favor and protect YOUR energy.

"Chill out; and stop worrying. All worry does is delay you."

Instead of worrying, surround yourself with people who encourage you, who make you happy, and who push you to keep going. Worrying delays you, but surrounding yourself with people who challenge you, will catapult you to the next best version of yourself.

"If you cannot be positive, then at least be quiet."

I'm sure you learned this lesson as a child. If you cannot be positive, then at least be quiet. Negativity doesn't know resolution. It's too busy pointing the finger, complaining about all that is 'wrong' to actually do whatever is necessary to reach a resolution. If you cannot be positive, do us all a favor and just hush.

"Just keep pushing."

This is easier to do when you link with people who believe in your shine, who love you enough to tell you the truth, and who aren't afraid to hold you accountable. That's the formula to keep you from running in place.

"Forgive your friends, you've forgiven your significant other for doing much worse."

Your friends are human, that means they make mistakes too. Don't lose a GOOD friend behind some bullsh–t. Forgive and drive on.

"GET STARTED."

You really CAN do anything you put your mind to. It won't be easy, but the hardest part is getting started.

"Do unto others as you would have them do unto you." Luke 6:31

Some don't worry about crossing others, since if they were you, they'd cross themselves too. It really is a blessing to be able to shift your gaze off of self, and onto others. When we do this, we practice compassion and empathy... which, in my opinion make us better people.

"Choose goals over gossip."

And surround yourself with people who choose goals over gossip too. Trust me, you won't regret this choice. Being in the know about this one's business, or that one's business won't put a dime in your pocket; it's a waste of time really. But when you sit at the 'GOALS' table, the conversation is different. The 'GOALS' table is where good connections and money are made.

"Do what the f-ck you say you're going to do."

Intentions don't move sh-t; ACTION does! People who don't honor their commitments aren't taken seriously. Don't commit if you can't follow through.

Section Five:

GENTLE REMINDERS FOR YOU, AND ANYONE ELSE WHO MAY NEED REMINDING.

"Exercise extreme caution when giving advice."

Especially if your advice wasn't solicited. And one other thing, before you give advice, think three times about whether you should even speak on whatever situation is being presented to you. Love the person confiding in your enough to say 'I can't tell you what to do, I have never been there or done that; what I can, and will do is pray for you though.'

"HE's intentional; never failing."

To be intentional is to live your life in such a way that every decision has a 'why' behind it. To be intentional is to choose to do, or not to do certain things based on the type of life you want to create. Know that GOD is intentional; and that his promises will never be broken. That means you can smile in the midst of any challenges knowing that it was all part of HIS plan to help promote you to the next best version of yourself.

"It's okay to choose yourself."

Sometimes, it's necessary to choose yourself. Don't let anyone manipulate you into feeling guilty for choosing yourself.

"A private life, is a happy life."

It's human nature to want to share whatever makes you happy with the world; BUT, be sure to exercise discretion. The reality is, not everyone deserves to witness your happy...some will curse it, the minute you let them in. Simply put, a private life is a happy life because it cuts down on the drama. Don't let social media fool you.

"You are only one person; the best you can do, is the best you can do."

You should remind yourself of this as often as necessary. People will try and pull you in a million different directions IF YOU LET THEM. It's important that you say 'yes' to the things that you want to say yes to,. . .and, that you're strong enough to say 'no' when you need to as well. Don't be guilted into doing anything you don't want to, just to please others.

"A general is only as strong as his soldiers."

No matter your position, you are no less significant than the CEO. He makes what he makes, because of all of the people who report to him. Social media tells everybody that you've got to be a 'Boss' to be important. Don't buy into this lie. A boss can't lead without direct reports.

"The quickest way to kill your happy is comparison."

Comparison kills motivation, which can in turn, halt your progress. Instead of comparing where you are against where the next person is, choose instead to celebrate how far you've come. Oh! And clap for those who are winning. Clap because you're happy for them, clap in anticipation of your win. You block your blessing when you don't.

"Let action move you, before words do."

I know you've heard the phrase 'actions speak louder than words.' Words should support what you have already demonstrated.

"It's important to be humble."

Be confident. Be confident, albeit humble.

"Conveniently leaving out material information is STILL a lie."

The same is true if you intentionally misrepresent material information. Some people will jump through a million and one burning hoops of fire just to circumvent telling the WHOLE truth; and, that a real shame too. Tell the truth and you don't have to have a good memory. It really is, just that simple.

"You will never be able to make everyone like you; but, you can leave them void of any sound reason to dislike you."

That is why it pays to take the high road. When you choose to be petty, you're only giving people more ammunition to come up with reasons why no one should deal with you.

"Letting go and giving up are not the same thing."

Don't let anyone manipulate you into believing that you gave up when you know you tried (with everything in you) to make things work. If you've exhausted every effort, and then choose to walk away, you didn't give up. YOU LET IT GO; Issa difference.

"The selfish will always lack."

Generosity brings abundance. Greater is he who is self sacrificing, helpful, giving and kind.

"In the end, walk has more clout than talk ever will."

So, don't worry about the talk so much. Instead, focus on the walk. Let your moves do the talking for you.

Section Six:

FIND A WAY, NOT AN EXCUSE. BE ACCOUNTABLE.

"You can't create a storm and then turn around and cry out to God when it rains."

I mean I guess you could, but don't expect much sympathy when you do. It's hard to look in the mirror and face the fact that the person staring back at you is the reason for your circumstances. But, the sooner you own the role you played in creating your storm(s), the closer you'll be to overcoming them.

"Life happens to all of us. You can be bitter or BETTER."

Choose BETTER, and start moving toward your idea of success.

"Accountability goes both ways. If you want to claim every victory, you've got to be willing to own every fail too."

This is easier to do when you take your Ls privately; learn from your mistakes and let your progress do the talking.

"Nothing can keep you down, if you refuse to stay down."

All too often we look for excuses as to why we didn't follow through on our commitments. Why we didn't accomplish this goal or that goal. Why we lack this or that, etc. The truth is, any answer outside of 'I' should have been more conscious, or "I" should have been more disciplined, anything outside of "I" is an excuse. We all have the same 24 hours as Jay and Bey; don't spend too much time licking your wounds (disappointments, upsets) feeling sorry for yourself. Bandage them up, identify the lessons learned, take a deep breath and then GET BACK UP.

"If you don't like something; change it."

If you are unhappy with your weight, make it a priority to exercise. If you are unhappy with your financial situation, make it a priority to manage the money you make, more efficiently. If you are a person who has trouble following through on your commitments, make it a priority to see your commitments all the way through to the end. You'll feel so much better when you stop talking about doing what you want to do. It won't be easy, but you should FIND a way.

"If you want to be taken seriously, you'll have to take yourself seriously first."

It's so important that you assume this mindset NOW. Until you take yourself seriously, no one else will.

"It's okay to expect what you give."

Standards and expectations are good as long as you bring
to the table, everything that you are commanding.

Opposition is nothing more than an opportunity to prove how well you know your sh-t."

Don't let the opposition disrupt your focus. Don't give the opposition the pleasure of seeing your foundation shifting.You might be scared sh-tless; but, nobody outside of you and God has to know that you're afraid. No matter how many times the opposition tries to interrupt your progress, KEEP GOING until you're done.

"There are consequences associated with every decision you make."

That's right. Every. Damn. Decision. Make sure you choose wisely.

"A person's weaknesses do not make them weak. His or her inability to face, and unwillingness to address said weaknesses does."

We all have weaknesses but, we shortchange ourselves when we choose to do nothing about them. Living the best version of yourself requires emotional, mental spiritual and physical fitness; and the only way you'll achieve that is through continual growth, learning and expansion.

Section Seven:

POSITIVE AFFIRMATIONS. PUT ONE, OR PUT A FEW IN THE AIR...

I am worthy.

I am enough.

I am able.

I deserve to be treated well.

I deserve to make mistakes
and to be forgiven for making
them too.

I deserve to love, and be
loved.

I am entitled to respect.

I am entitled to loyalty.

I am entitled to honesty.

52770097R00057

Made in the USA
Columbia, SC
11 March 2019